OUTSPOKEN
PAUL ROBESON
AHEAD OF HIS TIME: A ONE-MAN SHOW

CAROLE BOSTON WEATHERFORD

illustrated by **ERIC VELASQUEZ**

CANDLEWICK PRESS

In honor of my mother, Carolyn Whitten Boston,
a woman of strength and conviction
CBW

For my mother, Carmen Lydia Velasquez,
who introduced me to Paul Robeson's music
and the importance of his work as a humanitarian
EV

Italic text in poems indicates direct quotes from Paul Robeson or song lyrics; please see Source Notes for further information.

A genuine gift is like water; when it flows out it can never return.

—African proverb

ACT I—YOUTH

CRADLE SONG: DEEP RIVER

Two rivers course through my blood:
currents that rocked me before I was born.

One river is Resistance.
My great-great-great grandfather Cyrus Bustill
bought his way out of slavery, became a baker,
and, during the Revolution, baked bread
for General George Washington at Valley Forge.
In the early days of the new republic,
Cyrus cofounded the Free African Society,
the first human welfare organization for free blacks.
My mother's Quaker parents opposed war and slavery
and had ties to the Underground Railroad.

Steal away, steal away
Steal away to Jesus
Steal away, steal away home
I ain't got time to stay here.

My father, William, was born into slavery
on the Roberson plantation in North Carolina.
At age fifteen, he fled north to freedom.

No more auction block for me
No more, no more
No more slavery chains for me
Many thousand gone

One of my father's first acts as a free man
was to change his last name from the one
the slavers gave him to one of his own choosing—
   Robeson.
The Civil War broke out and President Lincoln signed
the Emancipation Proclamation, allowing black
   men to fight.
My father joined the US Colored Troops
to free his brothers and sisters still in bondage.
He never spoke of his years under the yoke.
Yet I bear the weight of that, too.

Two rivers course through my blood:
currents that rocked me before I was born.
One river is Resistance. The other is Intellect.
After freedom came, my father was studying
religion at Lincoln University when he met
my mother, Maria, a teacher. Her family boasted
scholars and artists. My parents' union
bore brilliant fruit: a physician,
a businessman, a minister, a schoolteacher,
and me—the youngest of seven children.

Two rivers rush through my blood:
Resistance and Intellect.
They converge
in my heart, run deep
in my soul.

Deep river . . .
Deep river, Lord.

◆

THE LITTLE BLACK BOY

Some things grown-ups remembered for me;
others I remembered for myself.

I do not remember my father in the pulpit
of all-black Witherspoon Street Presbyterian Church.
Like our community, our church was named
for a slaveholding past president of Princeton University.

I do remember that our community abutted the campus
and that a wrought iron gate locked African Americans out.
In Princeton, New Jersey, we were the servant class.

I cannot remember when, after more than twenty years
at the same church, my father was fired as pastor
and bought a horse and wagon to haul ashes
for other households. At three years old,
I did not feel the financial pinch or fathom the humility
that enabled my father, a college man, not only to take
the job of ashman in stride but to count it as a blessing.

I cannot remember that my mother helped my father
pen his sermons or that she joined him in visiting
the sick and in aiding the hungry, the jobless,
and the many migrants arriving from the South.
I cannot remember that my mother held me in her lap
or that her eyesight was so poor due to cataracts
that she bumped into the parlor stove and caught fire.
I was just six and not home when tragedy struck.
Shocked beyond recollection, I all but forgot my mother.
Yet the image of her in the coffin burned into my memory.

Nobody knows the trouble I've seen
Nobody knows my sorrow
Nobody knows the trouble I've seen
Glory, Hallelujah

I remember butter-and-sugar sandwiches for school lunch
and playing at homes of my black and white friends.
I was raised in the bosom of kin and caring neighbors
who fed me cornbread and mustard greens
and kept me while my father worked as a coachman
forty miles away at seaside resorts. I lost
my mother but gained a dozen second homes.
I cannot remember the years that I had her with me,
but I felt her absence when I saw my friends' mothers.

Sometimes I feel like a motherless child
Sometimes I feel like a motherless child
Sometimes I feel like a motherless child
A long way from home, a long way from home

I remember my older brothers and sister going off
to high school in Trenton or to boarding schools down south
because high schools in Princeton barred blacks.
I remember moving with my father to Westfield, New Jersey,
where he worked in Miss Fannie's grocery store,
I delivered groceries, and we lived in the store's attic.
While I attended an integrated school, my father found
a new flock and formed Downer Street AME Church.
At home, he preached academic perfection,
frowning upon my report card with six As but one B—
in Latin. He didn't care that I was the best in my class.
He expected more, and I did all I could to win his approval.
I loved my father more than anyone in the world.
That much I remember and hold on to.

◆

I GOT A HOME
IN THAT ROCK

When I was ten, my father called me. I ran from him.
Chasing me, he fell and lost his tooth.
I felt so guilty that I never again disobeyed him.
I worshipped my father. He was the bedrock
of my being, the grounds for my strength,
and the soil where my strivings took root.
In his eyes, I deserved the richest opportunities—

courses in history, literature, and the classics—
balanced with religious practice and African heritage.
My father did not care that Booker T. Washington,
the founder of Tuskegee Institute in Alabama,
urged blacks to focus on training for trades
rather than on book learning and social progress.
My father wanted more for his children—
the power of words and the freedom to think.

On weekdays I had instruction for the mind
and on Sundays, songs for the soul—
my father's sermons and African American spirituals.
At home, he played piano and we children
gathered around and harmonized. My father's voice
rose above the rest—a resounding touchstone.
I wish we could have held those notes forever.

Whether in a parsonage or a storefront attic,
I felt at home long as I was with my father.
One by one, my older siblings went off to college
or to launch their grown-up lives, leaving me
and my father at home together.
There was no card playing in our household,
but my father and I played checkers—
his favorite game—for hours on end.

◆

JOSHUA FOUGHT THE BATTLE OF JERICHO

I have my big brothers Reeve and Ben
to thank for my fighting spirit.
After Reeve dropped out of college,
my father got him a job as a hack driver.
Reeve had regular run-ins with the law
for standing up to racist whites who rode
in his carriage and disrespected him.
My father cast Reeve out for fear
that I would take up his ways.
Reeve's code stayed with me, though.
Don't ever take low. Stand up to them
and hit back harder than they hit you.
Reeve taught me to fight with my fists.

Joshua fit the battle of Jericho, Jericho, Jericho

Our household was a vocal training ground.
All of us joined in debates and in song.
From age eight, I was in the church choir.
At eighth grade graduation, I delivered
Patrick Henry's 1775 speech, "An Appeal to Arms,"
which called for revolution against British rule.
I breathed the power of my own convictions
into the patriot's famous last line:
Give me liberty or give me death.

Joshua fit the battle of Jericho, Jericho, Jericho

My big brother Ben, who played football
at Lincoln University, introduced me to that sport.
One of three blacks at a high school of 250 students,
and one of nine students in college prep courses,
I played fullback on the football team.
Fans cheered: *Let Paul have the ball! Yay—Paul.*
I was forward on the basketball team,
and shortstop and catcher on the baseball team,
and threw discus and javelin in track and field.
The music teacher trained my voice.
And the English teacher cast me as Shakespeare's Othello.

Joshua fit the battle of Jericho, Jericho, Jericho

Yet Mr. Ackerman, the racist principal,
had it in for me. If he hit me, I swore I'd hit back—
like Reeve taught me. Despite my 98 average,
Ackerman didn't want me to have a shot
at a college scholarship. So he failed to tell me
about the preliminary examination to qualify.
When I finally took the written test, I scored so high
that I won a scholarship to Rutgers University.

Joshua fit the battle of Jericho, Jericho, Jericho

At seventeen, I was only the third African American
admitted since the university's founding in 1766.
My hard-won scholarship was no welcome mat.
At football tryouts, racist bullies punched me,
broke my nose, dislocated my right shoulder,
and stomped on my hand, claiming five fingernails.
Though hurt, I fought back and made varsity.
Then I had to tackle racism from other teams.

Joshua fit the battle of Jericho
And the walls came tumbling down.

◆

MY MOUTH, MY MUSCLES, AND MY MIND

My father sent me to old Rutgers,
And resolv'd that I should be a man.

At Rutgers, I was driven by the thought
that my father expected me to excel.
So I plied the same tools that had propelled me
thus far: my mouth, my muscles, and my mind.
When I was broke, I'd put on one-man shows,
singing and speaking to hustle up fifty dollars.
I was chosen All-American in football
and earned a record fifteen varsity letters
in four sports: football, baseball, basketball,
and track and field.
A model student-athlete, I was inducted
into the Cap and Skull senior honor society
and won four oratorical contests—one with a speech
about unequal educational opportunities.

I knew about inequality firsthand.
Though my record at Rutgers was stellar,
my skin color made me an outcast.
In the glee club, I sang only on campus,
not on concert tours. And at the prom,
I was welcome only as a performer.

I sang from the balcony, apart from the partygoers,
and never once set foot on the dance floor.
I endured the denigration for a degree
that would make my father proud.
I only wish that he had lived to see me graduate.
First in my class, I was valedictorian and earned
a coveted key from the Phi Beta Kappa honor society.
By then, I was as sure of my strengths as I was
of the moral compass handed down from my father.
In my commencement address, I pledged myself
to the African American freedom struggle,
knowing that *our future lies chiefly in our own hands.*
I vowed to uplift *my untutored brother*
and to ensure *that neither the old-time slavery*
nor continued prejudice need extinguish self-respect,
crush manly ambition, or paralyze effort.

That summer, I moved to Harlem.

◆

9

ACT II—ARTIST

I WANT TO BE READY

Before my father passed, I had dashed his hopes
that I would follow him into the ministry.
Instead, I vowed to pursue a legal career.
He was disappointed but gave me his blessing.

With a law degree, I would battle injustice
all the way to the Supreme Court, if need be.
Columbia University's campus straddled
the Upper West Side and Harlem, the hub
of black culture at the dawn of the modern age.
But I was too swamped with studies to socialize.
Plus, I had to support myself in the big city.

To get by, on weekends during school, I applied my
athleticism to play for the Akron Pros
and the Milwaukee Badgers—teams
in the American Professional Football Association.
That was before the sport banned black players in 1933.
Summers on Rhode Island's seashore, I worked
at the whites-only Imperial Hotel in Narragansett.
Kitchen help, I washed dishes and peeled potatoes
and eventually rose the ranks to be a waiter.
On the beach, I exercised, working out
until my body resembled a bronze sculpture.

I want to be ready
I want to be ready

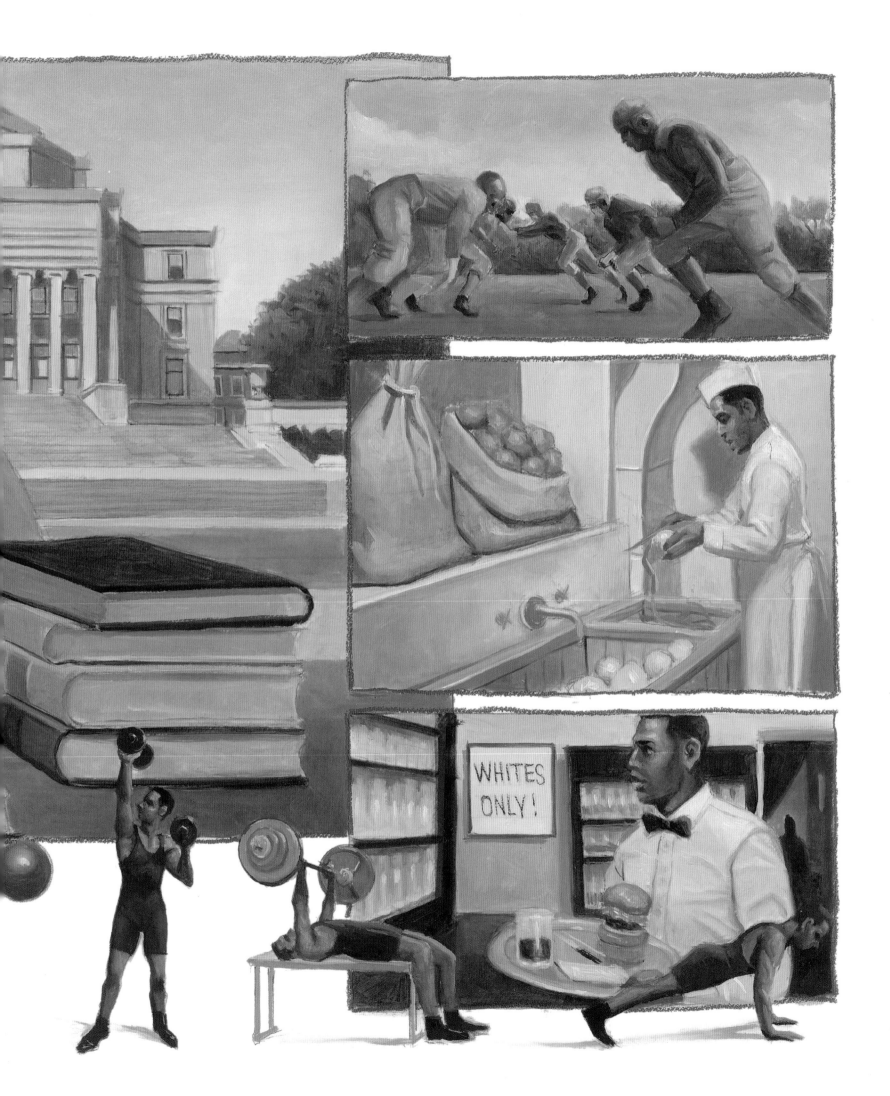

I also worked as a postal clerk and picked up
extra money onstage. I jazzed all-white audiences
at Harlem's Cotton Club, starred in the play
Simon the Cyrenian—about the African who carried
Jesus's cross—at the YMCA, and for one month
filled in for another singer in the Harmony Kings,
a vocal group featured in *Shuffle Along*,
an all-black musical revue on Broadway.

I had more careers back then than a cat has lives
and had less leisure than a honeybee.
I let off steam on the basketball court
and sprained my shoulder. In the hospital, I met
Eslanda Cardozo Goode, the first black analytical chemist
at Columbia Medical Center. She aimed to do research.
After only eight months, we married in 1921.
Essie attended my rehearsals and performances.
From the audience, she saw more in me
than I saw in myself—a future onstage,
brighter than that which law held.
She pushed me to pursue parts and set her own goals
aside so that I could quit my job and focus on performing.
The next year, the play that I was headlining went on tour,
and Essie and I honeymooned in England.
Although we experienced one slight at a hotel,
we were surprised by how little prejudice we faced.

I want to be ready
I want to be ready

After law school came a job at Stotesbury and Miner,
the all-white law firm of a Rutgers alumnus.
When I called a white secretary to take dictation,
she refused because I was black. I quit.
Luckily, another door had opened—the stage door.
Playwright Eugene O'Neill chose me for the lead
in *All God's Chillun Got Wings*. By then, I had starred
in academics, athletics, drama, and music.
With so many gifts and talents, my purpose
was hard to pinpoint. Then my life's work *found me*.
I belonged not in a courtroom or on a football field,
but onstage in the spotlight, bowing to applause.

◆

THIS LITTLE
LIGHT OF MINE

I strove for depth and dignity in each part I played,
even elevating parts endowed with neither quality.
A cast of complex characters, men of strength
and intellect often burdened with flaws.

In *The Emperor Jones*, I played Brutus,
a gambler and escaped convict who hops aboard
a ship to the Caribbean, where he preys
on superstitions to become the island's ruler.

In *All God's Chillun Got Wings*, I was Jim Harris,
a law student and half of an interracial couple.
The scene where the leading lady kisses my hand
sparked death threats from the Ku Klux Klan.

This little light of mine, I'm gonna let it shine.

In *Black Boy,* I was a drifter-turned-boxing champ
who falls from grace after lapsing into his old ways.
In *John Henry*—a musical drama inspired
by the folk hero—I played the title role.

John Henry was a steel-driving man,
Carried his hammer all the time,
And before he let that steam drill beat him down,
Said he'd die with his hammer in his hand

In *Show Boat,* set on the Mississippi River,
I was Joe, a dockworker. My number, "Ol' Man River,"
brought down the house and became my signature.
That role made me the toast of London society.

All over the world, I'm gonna let it shine.

In a revival of *Othello*, I had a second shot
at the same African character that I first played
on the high school stage. I had grown into him.
In one hundred years, only one other black man—
Ira Aldridge —had played the role on the English stage.
Once more, I was representing my people.
Like a true scholar, I mined ancient Roman oratory,
speeches by statesmen, and the Old English
and Middle English languages. I learned my lines
in five languages to sense differences in shading.
I poured mind, body, and soul into preparation.
Opening night, there were twenty curtain calls.
Thirteen years later, I took *Othello* to New York.
The show's 296 performances set a record
for the longest-running Shakespeare play on Broadway.
Othello is the part that I was born to play.

"Certain, men should be what they seem."

Let it shine, let it shine, let it shine.

◆

WE ARE CLIMBING JACOB'S LADDER

Oh, could I but express in song:
the cries of my ancestors under the yoke,
the simmering rage that racism provokes,
the joy and resilience and steadfast hope.

In London, I teamed up with Lawrence Brown,
a black, classically trained pianist, to perform
spirituals first sung by my enslaved ancestors.

We are climbing Jacob's ladder.
We packed concert halls at home and abroad
and brought the art form to white audiences:
soulful songs like "Deep River," "Swing Low, Sweet Chariot,"
and "We Are Climbing Jacob's Ladder."
We sold out New York's Carnegie Hall.
But we also performed for working people

in union halls, stadiums, and black churches.
The crowds begged for encores. We obliged them.

Every round goes higher, higher

Soon, my concert repertoire reached beyond
spirituals to include European arias and art songs,
folk melodies from many cultures and faiths,
as well as monologues from my theatrical roles.
I was part tour guide, part ambassador,
broadening audiences' vistas through song.

Rise, shine, give God the glory.

But I didn't stop at memorizing lyrics;
I worked with vocal coaches and learned
to sing in twenty foreign languages.
At home and abroad, my music crossed
boundaries and bridged cultures.
Record albums brought my voice into living rooms.
I even had my own company and label.
I called it Othello Records.

My mission became clear as a bell:
to *feed the people with my songs.*
Spirituals to illuminate the black plight,
Song of Freedom to reflect humanity's
shared struggles and strivings,
and "Ballad for Americans" to recall
democracy's promise of equal rights.
To voice resistance, I'd punch up lyrics.
My songs echoed my activism, spoke for all mankind.

I used *my art for myself, for my race, and for the world.*

◆

THE BLACK EMPEROR

ACTION!

My wife, Essie, who was my manager then,
got me my first film role—the lead in *Body and Soul*,
a silent movie by black filmmaker Oscar Micheaux.
I played an escaped convict posing as a minister.
Film was a powerful medium with the potential
       to project black pride. But movies more often
              reinforced racism by casting
                     African Americans
                            as beasts or buffoons.
                                   I shunned those parts,

instead seeking to play characters capable
of failings and flaws, goodness and grace.

For black actors in 1930s Hollywood,
dignified parts were rarer than leading roles.
But in British films—adventures, a World War I epic,
and a musical comedy—I landed a few plum parts,
from a dockworker, a coal miner, and a native guide
to African royalty. Some characters were gifted
with song, and others called to heroic sacrifice.

CUT!

Despite my best efforts to exalt blackness,
I played some roles that I am ashamed of.
In *Sanders of the River*, I was Bosambo,
an African leader and a strong ruler.
But during editing, the plot's thrust was changed
to justify imperialism and white superiority,
and Bosambo was reduced to a loyal servant.
In *Tales of Manhattan*—a braided story of a coat
that keeps changing hands—I played Luke, a sharecropper
who finds the garment with $43,000 in its pockets.

The scenes perpetuated plantation stereotypes.
Horrified by those movies, I offered money
to block their release. The producers declined.

In time, I insisted on approval of the final cut.
My contracts also included the unheard-of clause
that I not be required to travel in the South.
If I was denied the respect regarded white men,
I would at least demand star treatment.

Eventually, I'd had enough of seeing my image
exploited and contorted beyond recognition.
By 1942, I had made my last Hollywood film.
◆

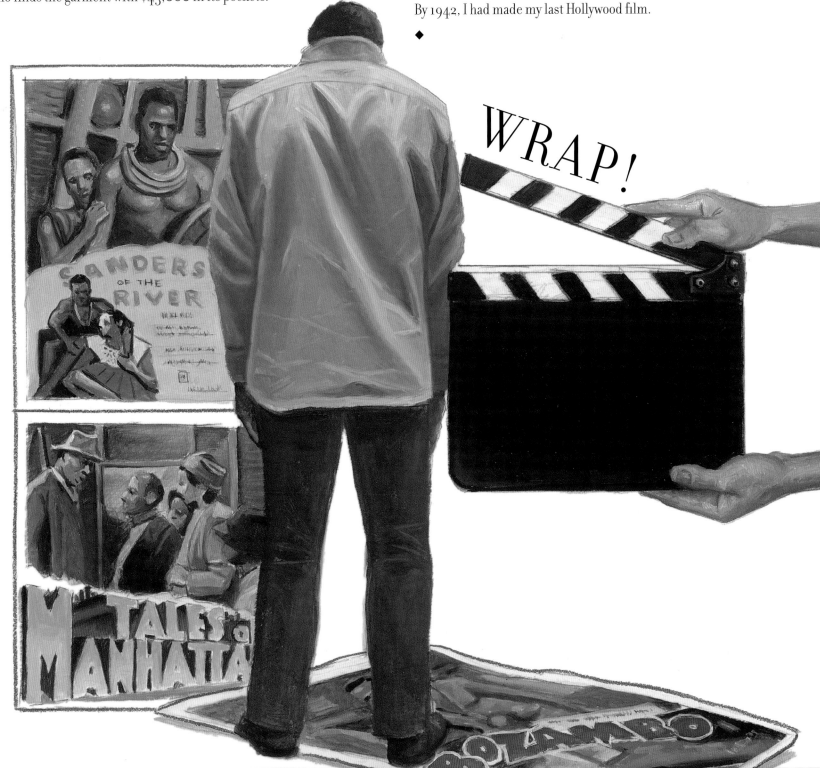

ACT III—ACTIVIST

THE UNITED NATIONS

My voice was a passport to the world.
In European capitals, I had the acceptance
that black men were denied in America.
I did suffer two slights, though. I was harassed
by Nazi guards in Berlin's train station and was barred
from a London hotel, which apologized for the scandal.
In the US, apologies for racism were unheard of.
Abroad, I found fertile ground for growth as an artist.
In 1928, Essie and I relocated to London.
For the twelve years that we lived overseas with our son,
Pauli, I did not just indulge in the culture; I dove in.

Let us break bread together on our knees

During the Spanish Civil War, a conflict
considered a dress rehearsal for World War II,
I did all I could to support the Republican struggle
against fascist general Francisco Franco.
I sang at hospitals and on the front lines
for the International Brigade volunteers

made up of troops from around the world.
I gave concerts to benefit Republican troops,
refugees of war, and exiled Spanish intellectuals.
By 1939, the world was on the eve of war.
My family and I returned to the United States.

Let us break bread together on our knees

World travel opened my eyes to social ills
on foreign soil. I was not just an international star
conveying the souls of black folk through song.
I was an emissary for universal struggles.

Wherever oppression reigned, I was in solidarity
with progressive movements. I dreamed of a world
where workers, the marginalized, and the colonized
united against poverty, racism, and imperialism.
A world where justice was the guidepost.
The world that I envisioned had not yet been born.
But I had to believe that it was on the horizon.

When I fall on my knees with my face toward
* the rising sun,*
O Lord, have mercy on me.

◆

LAND OF MY FATHERS

Way down in Egypt land

Years ago, my father told me that ancient
African kingdoms not only advanced civilization
but also attained greatness. Ever since, I yearned
to mine black heritage and to learn more
about political, social, and economic affairs
on the continent. To hear firsthand, I befriended
African students and workers living in England.
I met Kwame Nkrumah and Jomo Kenyatta,
who would later lead their homelands—Ghana
and Kenya—to independence from British rule.
I suddenly viewed the Motherland through African eyes
and saw myself as a symbol of all her descendants.
Essie and I studied African languages and culture.
In my heart, Africa was born anew.

Had I been born in Africa, I would have belonged,
I hope, to that family which sings and chants
the glories and legends of the tribe.

Oppressed so hard they could not stand

I felt compelled to advocate for Africa.
In 1935, fascist Italian leader Benito Mussolini—
on his conquest to rebuild the Roman empire—
invaded Ethiopia. The country had never been colonized.
Ethiopian emperor Haile Selassie asked the League of Nations
for help, but the West turned a blind eye and a deaf ear.
With a warrior's heart, I protested:
Ethiopians could do without the kind of "civilizing"
that European nations do with bombs and machine guns.
To foster national liberation movements in Africa,
I joined scholar and civil rights leader W. E. B. Du Bois
in founding the Council on African Affairs in the US.
Africa, I proclaimed, is for Africans.

Tell old Pharaoh
"Let my people go"

◆

IF I HAD A HAMMER
(HAMMER SONG):
THE LABOR MOVEMENT

In my years, I have worked as a postal clerk,
on docks and riverboats, and in brickyards,
hotels, and nightclubs. I inherited
my father's industry. As a boy, I saw him working
in the pulpit, at the grocery, and on the ash wagon.
To say nothing of the backbreaking labor
that he withstood during slavery.
I visited Welsh coal miners while filming
The Proud Valley, which was set in their community.
Their plight reminded me of my relatives,
sharecropping on tobacco plantations.
In my mind, the fights for workers' rights
and for racial equality were not just linked;
the two battles were one and the same.
I was no stranger to hard work or to workers.
I bonded with dock, railroad, and mill workers,
broke bread at their kitchen tables,
and sang with them around glowing campfires.
With laborers, I was among brothers and sisters.
The best way my race can win justice is, I believe,
by sticking together in progressive labor unions.

On the front lines of campaigns for workers' rights
and racial equality, I attended union meetings
and locked arms with workers on picket lines.
At factories and churches, in stadiums and squares,
I raised my voice—singing and giving speeches—
to rally workers in the auto industry,
in the Panama Canal Zone, and on pineapple plantations.
Several unions even named me an honorary member.
But my activism was not for show.
I was determined to help workers get a fair shake.
I knew that workers build nations.

FREEDOM

I understand why my brother Reeve flew off the handle
when degraded. Blacks faced ever-present reminders
that white racists deemed us beneath them.
Despite my international fame, I might be barred
from hotels, restaurants, and country clubs in the US.
When I was booked at the Hollywood Bowl in 1940,
every Los Angeles hotel refused me a room.
I wouldn't perform before segregated audiences—
the first American artist to take that stand.

I used my platform every way I could to push back
against racism. I spoke out against poll taxes,
fees that kept southern blacks from voting.
I called for equal employment opportunity
and pressed Major League Baseball to lift its ban
on black players. I advocated for the black residents
of Detroit's Sojourner Truth Housing Project.
And I took the stage at the Negro Freedom Rally
at Madison Square Garden in New York.
I did not revel in or squander my celebrity.
I used my platform to advance causes I believed in.

I suggested that African Americans retaliate against
the Ku Klux Klan and other violent hate groups.
I was twenty-one during the Red Summer of 1919
when white supremacists killed hundreds of blacks.
That same evil conjured the 1946 Moore's Ford lynchings.
In Georgia, a white mob fatally shot two young couples—
George and Mae Dorsey, and Roger and Dorothy Malcom.
No suspects were ever charged with the crimes.
I pressed for anti-lynching laws and enlisted others,
including physicist Albert Einstein, in the cause.
Through the American Crusade Against Lynching,
the organization that I founded, we took our fight
straight to President Truman. I was more radical
and less cautious than leaders of organizations
like the NAACP and the Civil Rights Congress.
Yet those groups saw that I played a vital role
as an unbending truth teller and troublemaker.
The NAACP awarded me the Spingarn Medal,
its highest honor. I believed in peace and brotherhood
but also in striking back if attacked.
If someone hit me on one cheek, I'd try to
   tear his head off
before he could hit me on the other one.
Perhaps my brother Reeve did rub off on me.

◆

NATIVE LAND
ПЕСНЯ О РОДИНЕ

If I flirted with communism,
it was because the Soviet Union
captivated me. The Soviets won me
with Article 123 of their constitution,
which barred racial discrimination—
at a time when segregation was legal in the US.

Reports from Claude McKay, a Harlem poet
and novelist, aroused my curiosity even more.
After visiting, Claude had nothing but praise
for the communist workers' state that taught
cultural diversity, promoted racial tolerance
and international brotherhood,
and opposed colonial rule in Africa and Asia.

During the Great Depression, thousands
of Americans answered the Soviets' call
for skilled workers to build a modern republic.
Black immigrants found good jobs
and fair treatment, then rare in the US.
I needed to see the Soviet Union for myself.
    In December 1934, Essie and I traveled there.
        On Soviet soil, the burden of racism

that I had carried all my life suddenly lifted.
Here I am not a Negro but a human being . . .
Here for the first time in my life,
I walk in full human dignity.
Pavel Robesona! Cheers welcomed me.
The Soviet system gave me hope that America
could live up to *its* promise of freedom for all.

I was so impressed that I enrolled my son,
Pauli, in boarding school in the Soviet Union
to shield him from American racism.
In return, I gave the Soviets moving renditions
of Russian folk songs, of their national anthem,
and of composer Isaak Dunayevsky's "Native Land."

◆

BALLAD FOR AMERICANS

My family fled Europe just as conflict erupted.
On board the ship, I flouted the dining room's
whites-only policy and declined the captain's invitation
to give a concert. Instead, I sang in the crew's quarters.
Back in New York, I returned to Harlem,
prepared to serve my people and my country.

On November 5, 1939, I sang "Ballad for Americans,"
a ten-minute pageant of American history,
live on the radio. The song's message of unity
resonated across cultural, social, and political lines.
After the broadcast, my popularity soared.

During World War II, I was as dedicated
to victory as any red-blooded American.
I toured defense factories promoting war bonds
and led Oakland shipyard workers in singing
"The Star-Spangled Banner."
I performed a concert for Negro soldiers
and sang battle songs on the radio.
On the first integrated USO tour,
I entertained troops on the front lines in Europe.

When Franklin Delano Roosevelt died
in 1945, my fellow actors chose me to read
Carl Sandburg's tribute to the late president.
With my deep voice and the poet's verses,
I tried to heal a grieving, war-weary nation.
I never stopped loving the United States.
But I love my people—black people—more.
I see America's beauty. Yet I see its failings, too.
Does that make me any less of a patriot?

◆

ALL MEN ARE BROTHERS

If I sympathized with the Communist Party in the US,
it was because they backed equality and workers' rights.
I needed to believe that a progressive labor movement
could pave the way for black liberation.
If I suggested at the Paris 1949 peace conference
that black Americans should not take up arms
in a war between the US and the Soviet Union,
it was because I had seen black troops
defend democracy in two world wars
only to return home to whites-only signs.

If I failed to denounce Soviet persecution of the Jews,
it was not because I did not have grave doubts
or because I had forgotten the ashen silence
at Auschwitz when visiting after the Soviets
liberated the notorious concentration camp.
If I was cordial to the Soviets throughout the Cold War—
the post–World War II standoff between the US
and the USSR—it was because the embrace
of Soviet audiences still warmed my heart.

I was flattered when the Soviet Union
named a mountain summit "Peak Robeson."

If anyone asks whether I am a card-carrying member
of the Communist Party, I feel no duty to answer.
I may be a *public* figure, but I am a *private* citizen.

If anything, I was loyal to a fault.

◆

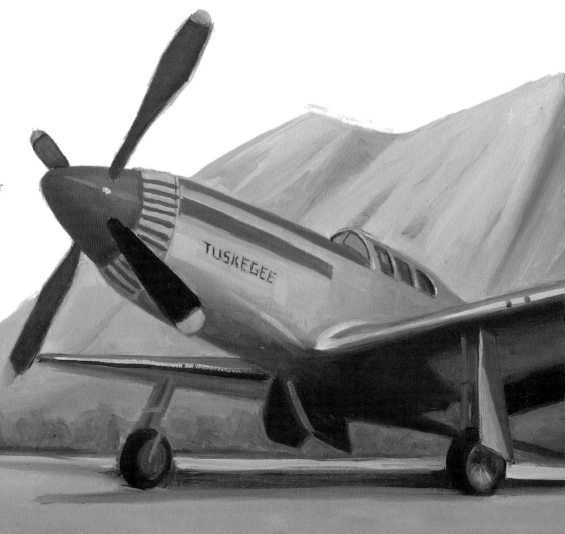

SCANDALIZE MY NAME

After World War II, the so-called red scare
turned public opinion against me.
For years, I had worked tirelessly
for left-wing labor and political movements.
Now my progressive leanings made me a target.
Senator Joseph McCarthy led the Congress's hunt
for communists and Soviet sympathizers.
The House Un-American Activities Committee,
HUAC for short, put my name on its blacklist,
branding me as a "Red" and deeming me
a danger to the welfare of the United States.
In 1949, eighty of my concerts were canceled,
but I kept my mission in the forefront.
The worst was yet to come, though.

Well, I met my brother de other day
Give him my right han'
Just as soon as ever my back was turned
He took an' scandaliz'd my name

In Peekskill, New York, a rampage broke out
before my concert. The mob hurled rocks,
overturned cars, trashed the stage,
punched concertgoers, and howled,
Go back to Russia, you niggers.
Days later, the American Legion, military veterans,
went on the attack at a second Peekskill concert.
More than 140 concertgoers were injured.

Some who had once heaped praise denounced me.
Former first lady Eleanor Roosevelt called
my concerts vehicles for communist propaganda.
And the NAACP's *Crisis* magazine
branded me a "Kremlin stooge."

Well, I met my sister de other day
Give her my right han'
Just as soon as ever my back was turned
She took an' scandaliz'd my name

Invitations were withdrawn, my biographies
were burned, my portraits were taken down,
my photographs were destroyed, and my name
was removed from All-American football teams.
I was not just being punished; I was being erased.

Worst of all, my passport was revoked.
Touring was my livelihood and my lifeline.
For eight years, I waged a legal battle
to regain the right to travel outside the US.
With my wings clipped, my income plummeted.
Still, I refused to sign a loyalty oath
swearing that I was not a communist.
From Harlem, I published a newspaper—*Freedom*.
Instead of muzzling me as intended,
the harsh penalty was for me a megaphone.
I became even more radical and outspoken.

Do you call dat a sister?
No, no! You call dat a brother?
No, no! Scandaliz'd my name

◆

IT AIN'T NECESSARILY SO:
OH, DIDN'T IT RAIN

Didn't it rain, chirrun
Talkin' bout rained
Oh, my Lord

By 1956, when I was called to testify before HUAC,
my views had hardened beyond compromise.
At the hearing, I was asked if I was now or ever had been a communist.
As far as I knew, the Communist Party was legal
and my political affiliation was *my* business.
Did the senators wish to trail me into the ballot box?
Repeatedly, I invoked the Fifth Amendment,
exercising my right not to testify against myself.

I was not allowed to give my prepared statement,
but I made my point.
I have struggled for years for the independence
of the colonial peoples of Africa.
When I am abroad I speak out against
the injustices against the Negro people of this land.
I am not being tried for whether I am a Communist,
I am being tried for fighting for the rights
of my people, who are still second-class citizens
in this United States of America.

You want to shut up every Negro
who has the courage to stand up and fight
for the rights of his people, for the rights of workers.

The success of a few Negroes, including myself,
can [not] make up . . . for thousands of Negro families
in the South. I have cousins who are sharecroppers,
and I do not see my success in terms of myself.
I have sacrificed literally hundreds of thousands,
if not millions, of dollars for what I believe in.

Why didn't I move to Russia? *Because my father*
was a slave, and my people died to build this country,
and I am going to stay here and have a part of it just like you.

Didn't it oh, oh my Lord
Didn't it rain?

◆

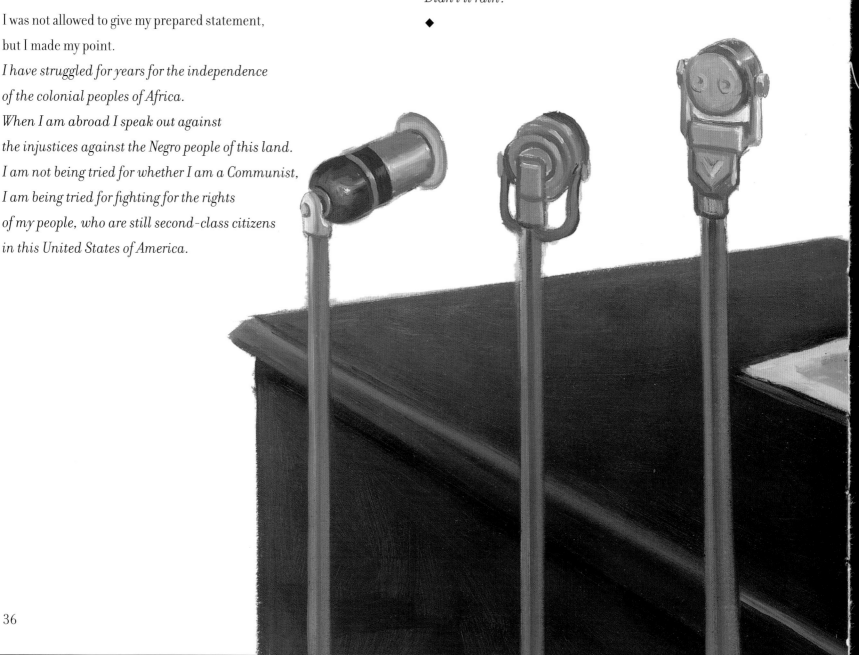

MOOD INDIGO

Since I couldn't travel abroad or book venues
in the United States, I sang at churches and union halls
and found clever ways around being blacklisted.
A makeshift recording studio in my brother's church
and concerts by phone or on the Canadian border.
I also published a book—*Here I Stand*—that compiled
my positions. "The time is now," I declared,
for "Negro action" to gain full freedom by 1963,
the centennial of the Emancipation Proclamation.
Black people had waited long enough for equality.
I dedicated my book to the Little Rock Nine,
the black students who integrated that city's public schools.
I also addressed the United Nations, accusing the US
of genocide for failing to outlaw lynching.
With the Civil Rights Movement underway,
black leaders had lost patience like I had long ago.
I suppose I was ahead of my time.

Feelin' tomorrow like I feel today
If I'm feelin' tomorrow like I feel today
I'll pack my truck and make my give-a-way

In 1958, after an eight-year court battle,
the US Supreme Court reinstated my passport,
ruling that it had been illegally withheld.
By then McCarthyism had fallen from favor
and I was free to rebuild my career.
Two months after a sold-out Carnegie Hall concert,
I set off on a European tour. Off and on for years,
I kept touring despite dark and jagged moods.
Then, in 1961, I fell mysteriously ill in Moscow
after a surprise party thrown for me at the hotel.
I locked myself in my bathroom, and overcome
by gloom, I hallucinated and slit my wrists.
My son suspected that American spies had drugged me.
Regardless, I was not the same afterward.
Following a hospital stay in Moscow, I was admitted
to a sanitarium in London. There, I was medicated
and received electroshock therapy over fifty times
until only a shell of the mighty Paul Robeson remained.
I was later treated at a clinic in East Berlin.
My health did improve, but not nearly enough.
My long run was over. The last curtain closed.
I never performed onstage again.

I hate to see that evening sun go down
I hate to see that evening sun go down

◆

38

ROCKIN' CHAIR

I have lived longer than I expected.
In the 1950s, I feared for my life.
I stay with family now—in seclusion.
I wonder: *What will history write of me?*

The artist must take sides.
He must elect to fight for freedom or slavery.
I have made my choice.
I had no alternative.

O Lord, I've done what you told me to do.
◆

Activist	Actor
African American	Artist
All-American	Athlete
Bass Baritone	Big Paul
Black Radical	Brother
Brutus	Citizen
Champion	Comrade
Communist	Conscience
Emperor Jones	Exile
Expatriate	Fighter
Gentleman	Gifted
Globe-trotter	Harlemite
Hero	Insane
Intellectual	Labor Organizer
Lawyer	Leader
Leftist	Letterman
Marxist	Militant
Musician	Negro
Ol' Man River	Orator
Othello	Patriot
Powerful	Preacher's Son
Princeton-born	Progressive
Renaissance Man	Scarlet Knight
Scholar	Singer
Six-foot-three	Socialist
Threat	Un-American?

Unparalleled.

TIME LINE

1898   April 9: Paul Leroy Robeson is born to Reverend William Drew Robeson and Maria Louisa Bustill Robeson in Princeton, New Jersey.

1904   January 20: Robeson's mother dies from burns suffered in a fire.

1910   Begins working as a kitchen boy, in shipyards, and in brickyards.

1915   Graduates from Somerville High School at the age of seventeen and wins a fully funded scholarship to Rutgers University in New Brunswick, New Jersey.

1917   Is selected for the All-American football team.

1918   Robeson's father passes away at the age of seventy-three.

1919   Graduates from Rutgers University as valedictorian and delivers his speech "The New Idealism."

Enrolls at New York University School of Law.

1920   Enrolls at Columbia University Law School.

Joins a group of students called the Amateur Players who produce plays on racial issues.

Makes his debut with the Amateur Players as Simon in Ridgely Torrence's *Simon the Cyrenian*.

1921   Marries Eslanda Cardozo Goode.

1922   Ends his football career after stints with the Akron Pros and the Milwaukee Badgers.

Makes his professional acting debut as Jim in the play *Taboo*.

1923   Graduates from Columbia University Law School.

Works at the law office of Stotesbury and Miner but quickly resigns due to racial tension.

1924   Lands the lead role in the play *All God's Chillun Got Wings*.

1925   Lands the lead role in the play *The Emperor Jones*.

Stars in his first film, Oscar Micheaux's *Body and Soul*.

1927   November 2: Paul Robeson Jr. is born.

1928   Performs in *Porgy* in New York and in *Show Boat* in London.

1930   Appears with his wife in the film *Borderline*. Robeson plays in the lead in Shakespeare's *Othello* in London.

1934   Enrolls in the School of Oriental and African Studies to study Swahili and phonetics. (A passionate linguist, he will learn twenty languages during his lifetime.) Robeson makes the first of many visits to the USSR to film a movie.

1935   Stars in the film *Sanders of the River*.

1936   The films *Show Boat* and *Song of Freedom* debut.

1937   The films *King Solomon's Mines*, *Jericho*, and *Big Fella* debut.

Robeson transforms the lyrics of "Ol' Man River" from a song of suffering to a song of defiance.

1939   November 5: Performs "Ballad for Americans" on live radio.

1940   The film *The Proud Valley* debuts.

1942   Declares that he will no longer act in Hollywood films.

1943   Stars in the Broadway production of *Othello*, which becomes the longest-running Shakespeare play on Broadway.

1945   Is awarded the Spingarn Medal by the National Association for the Advancement of Colored People.

1946   Meets with President Truman to demand his support for anti-lynching legislation.

1949   Addresses the Paris Peace Congress, rejecting fascism, racism, and imperialism and speaking against war.

August 27: In retaliation for Robeson's Paris Peace Congress speech, anti-communists brutally attack concertgoers during a scheduled performance in Peekskill, New York.

September 4: Robeson returns to Peekskill to perform, protected by a group of trade unionists.

1950   Is banned from television and has his passport revoked.

1952   Is accused of being a communist and is blacklisted in the United States.

1953   September 23: Is awarded the International Stalin Peace Prize.

1956   June 12: Is brought to testify before the House Un-American Activities Committee.

1958   April: Publishes his autobiography, *Here I Stand*.

April 9: India declares Paul Robeson Day a national holiday.

June: The United States government reinstates Robeson's passport.

1965   December 13: Paul's wife, Eslanda, passes away from cancer at age sixty-nine.

1973   Paul Robeson Jr. organizes a seventy-fifth birthday salute at Carnegie Hall. Coretta Scott King addresses the crowd.

1976   January 23: Paul Robeson passes away in Philadelphia.

SOURCE NOTES

p. 1, "Cradle Song: Deep River"

"Steal away . . . to stay here": "Steal Away," African American spiritual.

"No more auction . . . Many thousand gone": "No More Auction Block for Me," African American spiritual.

"Deep river . . . Lord": "Deep River," African American spiritual.

pp. 2–3, "The Little Black Boy"

"Nobody knows . . . Glory, Hallelujah": "Nobody Knows the Trouble I've Seen," African American spiritual.

"Sometimes I feel . . . a long way from home": "Sometimes I Feel Like a Motherless Child," African American spiritual.

p. 7, "Joshua Fought the Battle of Jericho"

"Don't ever take . . . they hit you": Stewart, 28.

"Joshua fit the battle . . . came tumbling down": "Joshua Fit the Battle of Jericho," African American spiritual.

"Give me liberty or give me death": Stewart, 32.

"Let Paul have the ball! Yay—Paul": Freedomways, 17.

pp. 8–9, "My Mouth, My Muscles, and My Mind"

"My father sent . . . be a man": "On the Banks of the Old Raritan," Rutgers alma mater, 1914.

"our future lies . . . paralyze effort": Ehrlich, 32.

pp. 10–12, "I Want to Be Ready"

"I want to be ready": "I Want to Be Ready," African American spiritual.

p. 14, "This Little Light of Mine"

"This little light . . . let it shine": "This Little Light of Mine," African American spiritual.

"John Henry was . . . in his hand": "John Henry," folk song.

"All over the world . . . let it shine": "This Little Light of Mine," African American spiritual.

"Let it shine . . . let it shine": ibid.

p. 16, "We Are Climbing Jacob's Ladder"

"Oh, could I but express in song": Leonid Dimitrievitch Malashkin, "Oh, Could I But Express in Song."

"We are climbing Jacob's ladder": "We Are Climbing Jacob's Ladder," African American spiritual.

"Every found goes higher, higher": ibid.

"Rise, shine, give God the glory": ibid.

"feed the people with my songs": Ehrlich, 57.

"my art for myself, for my race, and for the world": Stewart, 112.

pp. 20–21 "The United Nations"

"Let us break . . . on our knees": "Let Us Break Bread Together," African American spiritual.

"When I fall . . . mercy on me": ibid.

p. 22, "Land of My Fathers"

"Way down in Egypt land": "Go Down, Moses," African American spiritual.

"Had I been born . . . of the tribe": Ehrlich, 71.

"Oppressed so hard they could not stand": "Go Down, Moses," African American spiritual.

"Ethiopians could do . . . machine guns": Swindall, 75.

"Tell old Pharaoh 'Let my people go' ": "Go Down, Moses," African American spiritual.

p. 24, "If I Had a Hammer (Hammer Song): The Labor Movement"

"The best way . . . labor unions": "Paul Robeson: Internationally Acclaimed Performer, Champion of the People."

p. 26, "Freedom"

"If someone hit . . . the other one": Freedomways, 8.

p. 28, "Native Land / ПЕСНЯ О РОДИНЕ"

"Here I am . . . full human dignity": Duberman, 190.

pp. 34–35, "Scandalize My Name"

"Well, I met . . . scandaliz'd my name": "Scandalized My Name," African American spiritual.

"Go back to Russia, you niggers": Ehrlich, 85.

"Kremlin stooge": Alan, 572.

"Do you call . . . Scandaliz'd my name": "Scandalized My Name," African American spiritual.

p. 36, "It Ain't Necessarily So: Oh, Didn't It Rain"

"Didn't it rain . . . Oh, my Lord": "Didn't It Rain," African American spiritual.

"I have struggled . . . rights of workers": "Testimony of Paul Robeson."

"Because my father . . . just like you": ibid.

"Didn't it oh . . . Didn't it rain?": "Didn't It Rain," African American spiritual.

p. 38, "Mood Indigo"

"Feelin' tomorrow like . . . make my give-a-way": W. C. Handy, "St. Louis Blues," 1914.

"I hate to . . . sun go down": ibid.

p. 40, "Rockin' Chair"

"The artist must . . . had no alternative": Epitaph on Paul Robeson's gravestone.

"O Lord, I've . . . me to do": "I've Done What You Told Me to Do," African American spiritual.

BIBLIOGRAPHY

Alan, Robert [Brown, Earl]. "Paul Robeson—The Lost Shepherd." *The Crisis* 58, no. 9 (November 1951): 569–573.

Boyle, Sheila Tully, and Andrew Bunie. *Paul Robeson: The Years of Promise and Achievement*. Amherst: University of Massachusetts Press, 2001.

Duberman, Martin Bauml. *Paul Robeson*. New York: Alfred A. Knopf, 1988.

Ehrlich, Scott. *Paul Robeson: Singer and Actor*. New York: Chelsea House, 1988.

Francis, Matthew. "How Albert Einstein Used His Fame to Denounce American Racism." *Smithsonian Magazine*, March 3, 2017. www.smithsonianmag.com/sciencenature/how-celebrity-scientist-albert-einstein-used-fame-denounce-american-racism-180962356/.

Freedomways. *Paul Robeson: The Great Forerunner*. New York: International Publishers, 1998.

King, Gilbert. "What Paul Robeson Said." *Smithsonian Magazine*, September 13, 2011. https://www.smithsonianmag.com/history/what-paul-robeson-said-77742433/.

"Paul Robeson: Internationally Acclaimed Performer, Champion of the People." *The American Postal Worker*, December 31, 2015. https://apwu.org/news/paul-robeson-internationally-acclaimed-performer-champion-people.

Robeson, Paul. *Here I Stand*. New York: Othello Associates, 1958.

Robeson, Susan. *The Whole World in His Hands: A Pictorial Biography of Paul Robeson*. Secaucus, NJ: Citadel Press, 1981.

Simmons, Ann M. "Great Read: In Russia, Early African American Migrants Found the Good Life." *Los Angeles Times*, November 19, 2014. https://www.latimes.com/world/la-fg-c1-black-russian-americans-20141119-story.html.

Steinke, Nicole. "Paul Robeson: The Singer Who Fought for Justice and Paid with His Life." ABC Radio National (Australian Broadcasting Company), June 7, 2013. http://www.abc.net.au/radionational/programs/archived/intothemusic/paul-robeson/4691690.

Stewart, Jeffrey. *Paul Robeson: Artist and Citizen*. New Brunswick, NJ: Rutgers University Press, 1998.

Swindall, Lindsey R. *Paul Robeson: A Life of Activism and Art*. Lanham, MD: Rowman & Littlefield, 2013.

"Testimony of Paul Robeson before the House Committee on Un-American Activities, June 12, 1956." History Matters, http://historymatters.gmu.edu/d/6440/.

Yeakey, Lamont H. "A Student Without Peer: The Undergraduate College Years of Paul Robeson." *The Journal of Negro Education* 42, no. 4 (Autumn 1973): 489–503. https://doi.org/10.2307/2966562.

COPYRIGHT ACKNOWLEDGMENTS